GW00375227

Dorothy Day

Devoted Daughter of the Church

by
Fr Ashley Beck

*All booklets are published thanks to the
generous support of the members of the
Catholic Truth Society*

CATHOLIC TRUTH SOCIETY
PUBLISHERS TO THE HOLY SEE

Contents

Acknowledgements

I am grateful to Fr Martin Newell CP of the Catholic Worker Community in east London, and to Scott Albrecht of the Catholic Worker Farm in Hertfordshire for their advice and help; also to Philip Runkel, Archivist of the Department of Special Collections and Archives at Marquette University, Milwaukee, Wisconsin, and to the Anglican theologian Fr Ken Leech. Many subjects of biographical writings have left little of their own thoughts on paper. Dorothy Day, as a passionate journalist, was a prolific writer for nearly fifty years; often things she wrote are to be found in a number of different sources. I have quoted her extensively in this booklet as her own eloquent words give the best picture of her life.

ISBN 978 1 86082 507 1

A Modern-day Saint

In the year 2000 the Holy See recognised the cause for the beatification of Dorothy Day (giving her the title 'Servant of God'). Some years before Cardinal John O'Connor, Archbishop of New York, said in support of the process: 'It has long been my contention that Dorothy Day is a saint – not a 'gingerbread' saint or a 'holy card' saint, but a modern day devoted daughter of the Church'.

This booklet looks at the life of this woman, one of the most remarkable Catholics of the 20th century - as she has been described, 'probably the most fascinating witness to Christ that America has ever produced.'[1] Dorothy Day lived and worked as a left-wing journalist in Chicago and New York, converting to Catholicism and founding in the 1930s the *Catholic Worker* newspaper and the network of communities inspired by it. For the remaining fifty years of her life she witnessed consistently to Christ's love for the poor and the rejection of war and violence. For much of her life the values and causes she espoused were despised by many of her fellow Americans, including Catholics; now, over a quarter of a century after her death the strength of her witness goes far beyond the direct influence of the newspaper and movement she initiated in the 1930s. Much of the general philosophy – though not all the specific positions – of Dorothy Day is now in the mainstream of Catholic life, and this is why we can see her as a courageous prophet, anticipating the new directions in which the Holy Spirit has led the Catholic Church.

For the poor and for peace

The two pillars of Day's life and teaching bear this out – love for the poor and witness for peace. Day and her associate Peter Maurin established a radical form of love for the poor – living with the poor, sharing resources to help the poor, campaigning for poor workers and the homeless - following in the footsteps of many saints in the history of Christianity. Since the Second Vatican Council, and partly as a result of the 'theologies of Liberation' the notion of the *preferential option for the poor*, categorically endorsed in the teachings of Pope John Paul II, has become central to the social teaching of the Church.[2] No one would deny that the Church has still a long way to go before it lives out fully this commitment in faithfulness to the gospel, and many Catholics in affluent countries either do not know about this commitment or refuse to accept it, but it is clear that there has been an enormous shift in thinking since the *Catholic Worker* newspaper was founded in 1933.

This is just as true with regard to Day's teaching and witness for peace. For her and many in the Catholic Worker movement this took the form of *absolute pacifism* (for example, opposing American involvement in the Second World War), and being imprisoned for non-participation in Civil Defence exercises, together with the burning of draft papers. This stance became even more important in the USA during the Vietnam War of the 1960s, influencing figures such as Daniel Berrigan and Thomas Merton. While the Catholic Church has not espoused an absolute pacifist position (and it has not been held by everyone in the Catholic Worker movement) since the Second World War and the pontificate of Blessed John XXIII the Catholic Church has become explicitly opposed to war[3]. This development is continuing all the time, as we can see from the strong opposition to nuclear deterrence from Pope Benedict XVI. Unquestioning patriotism and support for militarism on the part of the Church, so widespread seventy years ago both in the US and Europe, and so opposed by Day, is now the 'quirky' position for Catholics to hold, not that of the mainstream.

As the cause for her beatification progresses it is right for us to assess her influence and reflect on her heroic qualities. We should, however, recall that she herself said: 'Don't call me a saint. I don't want to be dismissed so easily.'

Early Life

Dorothy Day was born on 8 November 1897 in Brooklyn, New York. Her father, John Day, was a sports journalist – the nature of his work meant that the family moved large distances across the United States during Dorothy's early life: she, and her brothers Donald, Sam and John followed him into journalism (although she never wrote about sport). In her autobiographical memoir *The Long Loneliness* Day makes it clear that her father's long working hours, on night shifts, made him a distant figure in the family.[4]

His family was from Tennessee; the family of her mother, Grace Satterlee, came from New York State. When Dorothy was very young the family moved to California, where they lived happily, and in some comfort, until the cataclysmic event of the San Francisco earthquake in 1906. This event did enable her to appreciate how people could help others in adversity: 'Another thing I remember about California was the joy of doing good, of sharing whatever we had with others after the earthquake, an event which threw us out of our complacent happiness into a world of catastrophe.'[5]

To Chicago

Her family did not have long to experience this positive side: her father's newspaper plant burnt down as a result of the earthquake so he lost his job and the family promptly moved to the mid-west, settling in Chicago. She had not been brought up in a religious family and had not even been baptised; but in Chicago she did encounter religious people and the Bible. A Catholic neighbour whom she once found deep in prayer made a big impression on her, as this account of a time when Dorothy was looking for the woman's daughter shows:

> 'In the front bedroom Mrs Barrett was on her knees, saying her prayers. She turned to tell me that Kathryn and the children had all gone to the store and went on with her praying. And I felt a warm burst of love toward Mrs Barrett that I have never forgotten, a feeling of gratitude and happiness that still warms my heart when I remember her. She had God, and there was beauty and joy in her life. All through my life, what she was doing remained with me.'[6]

By the time she was twelve years old the family had moved to a prosperous area of Chicago and she had encountered the life of local Episcopalian parishes, loving the beauty of their liturgy and music; so in due course she was baptised and confirmed as a member of the Episcopal

Church. From this early age the Psalms made a big impression on her: 'Whenever I felt the beauty of the world…. in the material universe around me, or glimpsed it in human love, I wanted to cry out with joy.'[7]

University and journalism

She also at this early age read the sermons of John Wesley. Although Dorothy was not close to her father (and in later life they clashed bitterly and were not even reconciled when he died), his influence was important in many ways. He would not have 'trashy' novels in the house, so his daughter avidly read the classics of English and French literature. She also encountered the influential writings of Sinclair Lewis.[8] She was aware at this early age of social problems and this had an abiding effect on her.[9] At the age of sixteen she won a scholarship to the University of Illinois. Perhaps surprisingly her experience at university was negative – although she read avidly (especially from now on Russian authors – Gorky, Chekhov, and Tolstoy and, above all, Dostoyevsky) she avoided campus social life and worked in order to support herself financially. She began her journalistic career writing for local papers and joined the Socialist Party. Her growing anger at social injustice made her disillusioned with religion, as she wrote later:

'Why was so much done in remedying the evil instead of avoiding it in the first place? Disabled men, men without arms and legs, blind, consumptive, exhausted men with all the manhood drained from them by industrialism; farmers gaunt and harried with debt; mothers weighted down with children at their skirts, in their arms, in their wombs, and the children ailing, rickety, toothless – all this long procession of desperate people called out to me. Where were the saints to try and change the social order, not just to minister to the slaves but to do away with slavery?...Our Lord said, "Blessed are the meek", but I could not be meek at the thought of injustice. I wanted a Lord who would scourge the moneylenders out of the temple, and I wanted to help all those who raised their hand against oppression. Religion, as it was practiced by those I encountered, had no vitality. It had nothing to do with everyday life; it was a matter of Sunday praying. Christ no longer walked the streets of this world. He was two thousand years dead and new prophets had risen up in His place.'[10]

Many a Christian brought up in an affluent parish has felt this same sense of alienation, now as then. This is what she wrote later about how other people's religious faith put her off:

'There was no attack on religion because people were generally indifferent to religion. They were neither hot nor cold. They were the tepid, the materialistic, who hoped that by Sunday churchgoing they would be taking care of the afterlife, if there were an afterlife. Meanwhile they would get everything they could in this.'[11]

New York, political activist

Day's journalism and social activism soon outweighed her academic studies, and she dropped out of university after two years when her family moved to New York in 1916. But she had made deep and influential friendships, such as that with Rayna Simons. She and her future husband Samson Raphaelson were Jewish, and the way they were treated at university was Day's first encounter with anti-semitism – in the 1930s, she would found the first Catholic group opposed to anti-semitism. The importance of this friendship lies partly in the encouragement Day received for her aspirations as a writer:

'It was a short story I have sent to the university paper that made me a part of Rayna's group. She became as enthusiastic about my writing as she was about Raph[aelson]'s and when I became moody and temperamental she drew me out of myself by her vivid interest in all that concerned me.'[12]

Rayna later went to Moscow and died of cancer in 1927. Dorothy was by 1916 a chain smoker and her radical politics set her very much at odds with her father, and they could not easily share the same home, so she moved into her own apartment in New York and got her first proper job with *The Call*, a Socialist newspaper, linked to the American Federation of Labour and the Industrial Workers of the World (I.W.Ws, or 'Wobblies'), coming under the influence of Mike Gold and Peggy Baird. Industrial relations were very polarised in the United States at that time, and this increased further after the Russian Revolutions in 1917 and the entry of the United States into the war in 1917. The fall of the Tsar of Russia prompted a massive demonstration in Madison Square which Day attended in exhilaration.[13] She was naturally part of movements which opposed America's entry into the war shortly after that resisting conscription and she got a job with a magazine called *The Masses*. This was closed down by the government and its editors charged with sedition. All these groups were under constant surveillance by the police. Among friends she made from this period was Elizabeth Gurley Flynn, the future leader of the American Communist Party.[14] This was also when Day first encountered *anarchism*, a political outlook which remained constant throughout her life. Anarchism is a complex and often misunderstood outlook. This is what she writes in *The Long Loneliness*:

'Anarchism, according to the American Encyclopaedia, is a vaguely defined doctrine which would abolish the state "and other established social and economic institutions and establish a new order based on free and spontaneous co-operation among individuals, groups, regions and nations. Actually anarchism is not one doctrine but many; practically every theoretical anarchist has had his own distinctive ideas."....

Anarchism has been called an emotional state of mind, denouncing injustice and extolling freedom, rather than a movement. There was anarchism in ancient Greece. Zeno believed that freedom and equality would bring out the essential goodness of human nature. Kropotkin looked back to the guilds and cities of the Middle Ages, and though of the new society as made up of federated associations, co-operating in the same way as the railway companies of Europe or the postal departments of various countries co-operate now…

Kropotkin wanted much the same type of social order as Eric Gill, the artist, Father Vincent McNabb, the Dominican street preacher, G. K. Chesterton, Hilaire Belloc and other distributists advocated, though they would have revolted at the word anarchist, thinking it synonymous with chaos, not "self-government" as Proudhon defined it. Distributism in the English term for that society whereby man has sufficient of the world's goods to enable him to lead a good life. Other words have been used to describe this theory, mutualism, federalism, pluralism, regionalism; but anarchism – the word, first used as a taunt by its Marxist opponents, best brings to mind the tension always exiting between the concept of authority and freedom which torments man to this day.'[15]

Christian anarchism

What this shows is where Day's view of Christian anarchism, as she developed it alongside Peter Maurin in later years, fits into the overall Christian tradition. The social teaching of the Catholic Church does not take the same view of the role of the state[16], and yet there are points of contact between these outlooks and the concept of *subsidiarity* as expounded by Pope Pius XI in his encyclical *Quadragesimo Anno* in 1931, and Day and Maurin always argued that they were being faithful to the pope's vision.

Another important cause was the struggle for women to be given the vote, and it was while she was protesting outside the White House in Washington with other women suffragists that she was arrested and imprisoned for the first time (as an anarchist, when women in the

USA were later given the vote Day did not exercise this right). She and the other prisoners went on hunger strike to claim the rights of political prisoners – eventually this was granted. At her darkest moments during the imprisonment Day was comforted by the Psalms:

'I began asking for a Bible the second day I was imprisoned, and by the fourth day it was brought to me. I read it with the sense of coming back to something of my childhood that I had lost. My heart swelled with joy and thankfulness for the Psalms. The man who sang these songs knew sorrow and expected joy… (*Psalm 125* [*126*] *follows*)

If we had faith in what we were doing, making our protest against brutality and injustice, then we were indeed casting our seeds, and there was the promise of the harvest to come.'[17]

Imprisonment

Day was often imprisoned during her life and her sense of solidarity with prisoners was consistently strong, as was her opposition to the brutality of the death penalty.

This experience and the atmosphere of the war years led to a sense of drift in Day's life, accentuated by the suicide of one of her friends. Among them there was a great sense that the revolution was coming:

'We lived in one world, and it was a world in which dreams came true, where there was a possibility of workers being able to take over the means of production and starting to build that kind of society where each received according to his need and worked according to his ability.'[18]

At the same time the life and spirituality of the Catholic Church was not far away:

'It was on these cold bitter evenings that I first heard "*The Hound of Heaven*," in an atmosphere of drink and smoke. Gene[19] could recite all of Francis Thompson's poem, and would sit there, black and dour, his head sunk as he intoned, "And now my heart is as a broken fount, wherein tear droppings stagnate." The idea of this pursuit by *The Hound of Heaven* fascinated me. The recurrence of it, the inevitableness of the outcome made me feel that sooner or later I would have to pause in the mad rush of living and remember my first beginning and my last end.

Many a morning after sitting all night in taverns or coming from balls at Webster Hall, I went to an early morning Mass at St Joseph's Church on Sixth Avenue and knelt in the back of the church, not knowing what was going on at the altar, but warmed and comforted by the lights and silence, the kneeling people and the atmosphere of worship'[20]

Affair and abortion

As part of how she responded to this in the last few months of the war Dorothy signed up as probationer nurse at the King's Country hospital in Brooklyn, confident that by doing this she was not aiding the war effort, but rather war's victims. The year she spent doing this combined a great sense of compassion for the patients with a vigorous regime of hard work and difficult relationships with others on the wards.

At the end of her time in the hospital she formed a tumultuous relationship with a hospital orderly, Lionel Moise. She fell in love with him and after they both left the hospital they moved into an apartment together in Manhattan. It was a stormy love affair – after their first separation Day attempted suicide.[21] One feature of her specifically autobiographical writings is a tendency to avoid very painful or difficult episodes in her life: consequently the main source for this period is the semi-autobiographical novel she wrote in 1924, *The Eleventh Virgin* (which she came to hate; it is also very hard to obtain[22]). Although as a committed socialist Day was involved in campaigning for 'birth control rights' (covering in her journalism the imprisonment of activists in that cause) she became pregnant by Moise. Rather late in her pregnancy, because the relationship was far from stable and she was afraid of losing him, she decided to have an (illegal) abortion:

'According to Dorothy's novel, the operation occurred in an apartment in the Upper East Side. A surgical instrument cut the child from the lining of her womb. For several hours there were painful contractions, one spasm every three minutes. Finally, a half year old child was born dead.'[23]

This did not save the relationship, and Moise left her immediately afterwards, although they were later reunited in Chicago.

Doomed marriage

She then, 'on the rebound', married in early 1920 a wealthy writer, Berkeley Tobey, who lived in a large apartment in Greenwich Village. Again there are few details about this in her writings. The couple did go to Europe for some months, visiting London and Paris, and they spent 6 months on the Italian island of Capri: for the rest of her life Italian cooking would always remind her of this time. It seems as if she was still in love with Lionel Moise; during this period she wrote *The Eleventh Virgin*, but by the summer of 1921 her marriage to Tobey was over[24].

By 1922 she was living in Chicago and working on a paper called *The Liberator*. Women linked to the I.W.W. were treated by the police as if they were prostitutes and Dorothy was arrested after one of the so-called 'Palmer Red Raids' which were such a feature of life in America in these turbulent years.[25] Dorothy was shocked by the ways in which the women prisoners were abused and humiliated: '.... It was an unutterably horrifying experience for me. I had opened the door in fear and trembling and had been forced to dress practically in the presence of two detectives, leering....'

She also lived with Catholic girls in Chicago who went to Mass and set aside times for prayer each day. The Catholic Church was fascinating to Day, who wrote: 'worship, adoration, thanksgiving, supplication...were the noblest acts of which we are capable in this life.'

Relationship with Forster Batterham

After this she moved to New Orleans with her friend Mary Gordon and lived near St Louis Cathedral. Catholicism again came into her life; she bought a rosary and often went to Benediction at the cathedral.

In 1924 *The Eleventh Virgin* was published. She later said of this 'I wrote a very bad book'[26] and did not receive much in royalties. However, the publishers did sell the film rights for the book and she got half of the sum for this, then the princely sum of $2,500.[27]

With this money she moved back to New York and bought a small fisherman's cottage on the coast of Staten Island. This remained one of her favourite places for the rest of her life. It was part of a 'colony of artists and radicals'[28] and she began one of the most important personal relationships of her life, with Forster Batterham.

He was a biologist of English descent with a strong interest in the natural sciences. They began to live together, and Dorothy, having lived all her life in cities, began to appreciate things such as the stars and the shells on the beach where they lived. She wrote later:

> 'I had known Forster a long time before we contracted our common-law relationship, and I have always felt that it was life with him that brought me natural happiness, that brought me to God. His ardent love of creation brought me to the Creator of all things. But when I cried out to him, "How can there be no God, when there all these beautiful things," he turned from me uneasily and complained that I was never satisfied. We loved each other so strongly that he wanted to remain in the love of the moment; he wanted me to rest in that love. He cried out against my attitude that there would be nothing left of that love without a faith.'[29]

Tamar is born

For this happiness and time for reflection rekindled all her religious feelings, and it was precisely this which drew her further away from Batterham, along with his resistance to conventional marriage or family life, accentuated when Dorothy became pregnant again and gave birth to a daughter, Tamar Teresa[30], on 4 March 1926, by which time she was praying regularly (talking to Our Lady while doing the housework) and filled with a deep love for God[31]. The birth brought great joy:

> 'When the little one was born, my joy was so great that I sat up in bed in the hospital and wrote an article for the *New Masses* about my child, wanting to share my joy with the world. I was glad to be write this joy for a workers' magazine because it was a joy all women knew, no matter what their grief or poverty, unemployment or class war.'[32]

This birth would begin the process of ending her relationship with Tamar's father and mark an important stage in her spiritual search:

> 'Supper always was early and the baby comfortably tucked away before it was dark. Then, tired with all the activities that so rejoiced and filled my days, I sat in the dusk in a stupor of contentment.
>
> Yet always those deep moments of happiness gave way to a feeling of struggle, of a long silent fight still to be gone through. There had been the physical struggle, the mortal combat almost, of giving birth to a child, and now there was coming the struggle for my own soul. Tamar would be baptised, and I new the rending it would cause in human relations around me. I was to be torn and agonised again, and I was all for putting off the hard day.'[33]

Conversion and Life as a Catholic

Dorothy had met a nun on the beach at Staten Island, and with her help had Tamar Teresa baptised in July 1927. This nun, Sister Aloysia of the Sisters of Charity

> 'had had none of the university summer courses that most Sisters must take nowadays. She never talked to me of the social encyclicals of the Popes. She gave me a catechism and brought me old copies of the *Messenger of the Sacred Heart*, a magazine which, along with the Kathleen Norris type of success story, had some good solid articles about the teachings of the Church. I read them all; I studied my catechism; I learned to say the Rosary; I went to Mass in the chapel by the sea; I walked the beach and I prayed; I read the *Imitation of Christ*, and St Augustine, and the New Testament.'[34]

Sister Aloysia was not a gentle teacher – she was very critical of Dorothy's domestic skills – but she was thorough in the grounding she gave her in the Catholic faith as it became clear that after the child's baptism Dorothy would become a Catholic.

'Tamar was baptised in July. We went down to Tottenville, the little town at the south end of the island; there in the Church of Our Lady, Help of Christians, the seed of life was implanted in her and she was made a child of God.'[35]

Ties being cut

Forster Batterham prepared a delicious meal for everyone afterwards but made sure he was not around to share it; relations deteriorated in the next few months and he left Dorothy and the baby on a number of occasions in the following months.[36] This was a very difficult period as she saw her relationship with him fall apart; it was made worse by the pain and anger they both felt at the unjust execution by electrocution of two anarchists, Nicola Sacco and Bartolomeo Vanzetti:

'Throughout the nation and the world, the papers featured the struggle for the lives of these two men….the day they died, the papers had headlines as large as those which proclaimed the outbreak of war. All the nation mourned. All the nation, I mean, that is made up of the poor, the worker, the trade unionist – those who felt most keenly the sense of solidarity – that very sense of solidarity which made me gradually understand the doctrine of the Mystical Body of Christ whereby we are members one of another.'[37]

Becoming a Catholic

The pain from this, the disintegration of the relationship and an illness suffered by Day meant that she did not become a Catholic until the very end of the year, 28 December, when she was baptised conditionally at Tottenville, receiving also the sacraments of Penance and the Eucharist.[38] Often accounts of conversion to the Catholic faith are filled with joy and exhilaration, but in Day's case the initial experience is depicted by her as being rather mechanical and grim, 'and certainly with no consolation whatever'[39] The reason for this is not hard to see. Not only was her conversion costing her the relationship she had cherished with the man she loved, the father of her child; she knew too that it was a step away from the campaigning and journalistic work for social justice which had been the mainstay of her life. Among anarchists and communists in the USA of the late 1920s, the Catholic Church was perceived, not inaccurately, as being on the 'wrong side' in the struggle of the poor and the oppressed in history. She knew, correctly, that she was joining the Church of the masses, of the immigrants, of "Irish cops and washerwomen", as her father scornfully put it[40] (and this remains true today). But at the same time

'…here I was going over to the opposition, because of course the Church was lined up with property, with the wealthy, with the state, with capitalism, with all the forces of reaction. This I had been taught to think and this I still think to a great extent…

I certainly believed this, but I wanted to be poor, chaste and obedient. I wanted to die in order to live, to put off the old man and put on Christ…'[41]

Searching for her vocation

In the first months and years of her life as a Catholic she had a lot to work through. On the advice of her confessor she remained for a time working for the Communist Anti-Imperialist League. After a period of working with the Catholic Fellowship of Reconciliation in New York, she and Tamar moved to California having got a screen-writing job with Pathé in Hollywood. This proved less successful than she had imagined, and subsequently they lived for a time in Mexico, Dorothy's first experience of living in a Catholic country.[42] In these first four or five years as a Catholic Dorothy was searching for a vocation and trying on her own to bring up a baby. Although she had many friends in New York, her period in Los Angeles was very lonely; she also suffered periods of illness. At the heart of this search was the question of how to live out her commitment to the poor and the oppressed within the family of the Catholic Church. By late 1932 she was writing for the Catholic journal *Commonweal*, and went to Washington to cover the enormous Hunger March for the Unemployed, a big demonstration in the midst of the Depression organised by Communists. She reflected later on how she felt:

'How little, how puny my work had been since becoming a Catholic, I thought. How self-centred, how ingrown, how lacking in sense of community! ... I watched my brothers in their struggle, not for themselves but for others. How our dear Lord must love them, I kept thinking to myself. They were His friends, His comrades, and who knows how close to His heart in their attempt to work for justice...'[43]

The dislocation she felt is not uncommon among converts looking for a true home within the Catholic Church; but she felt it more keenly than most. She was conscious that while she was now writing for Catholic publications, and had got to know quite a few priests, she was not part of a community, and 'still did not know personally one Catholic layman.' At the end of the demonstration, on the feast of the Immaculate Conception, she prayed for guidance at the national shrine at the Catholic University: 'There I offered up a special prayer, a prayer which came with tears and with anguish, that some way would open up for me use what talents I possessed for my fellow workers, for the poor.'[44]

When she got back to New York she met a Catholic layman who would influence her more than anyone else she had known. His name was Peter Maurin.

Peter Maurin

'When people come into contact with Peter....they change, they awaken, they begin to see, things become as new, they look at life in the light of the Gospels. They admit the truth he possesses and lives by, and though they themselves fail to go the whole way, their faces are turned at least toward the light.'[45]

In her apartment was waiting for her a French peasant[46],

'a short, stocky man in his mid-fifties, as ragged and rugged as any of the marchers I had left. I like people to look their part, and if they are workers, to look like workers, and if they are peasants to look like peasants...'[47]

He introduced himself as Peter Maurin (pronouncing the name as if it were English, not French) and said that he had been advised to make himself known to Day by George Shuster, the editor of *Commonweal*.[48] That evening and the following day he began a process of educating Day in the Catholic faith more fully, or 'indoctrinating' her, as he put it. While this term has negative connotations today, Maurin was unashamed about using the term, sharing the doctrines of the Catholic

Church as interpreted by him and applied to everyday life. The other phrase he used to describe these teaching exercises, with Day and with others, was the 'clarification of thought'. Before looking at the effects of this teaching, we should look at the life of this remarkable man before Dorothy Day met him in her New York apartment in late 1932. The details are sketchy, because Maurin was interested more in ideas than in people; he left no autobiographical writings and what is known had to be teased gradually out of him by Day and others – and there are quite a few gaps. Professor Sicius for his publication of Day's biographical work did visit Maurin's home village in France and met a number of members of his large family.[49]

Maurin's background

Pierre Joseph Orestide Maurin was born on 9 May 1877 in the small village of Oultet, in the Languedoc region of southern France.[50] It is a tiny village and his family was large – the family lived very simply from what they grew and reared; people were healthy and lived to a great age.[51] The influence of this simple, self-contained way of life on Maurin's subsequent thinking and teaching cannot be exaggerated: all his life he maintained a belief in the importance of manual work in the country, and a suspicion of industrial work in cities and this was a source of tension, sometimes creative, with Day.

In his teens he entered the community of the Christian Brothers in the town of Mende. He spent some years in the community teaching, but never took final vows. His time with them was disrupted by enforced secularisation as a result of the rift between the Church and the French Third Republic, and the closure of many of the order's schools.

In spite of this rift the late 19th century was an important time in the development of Catholicism in France, at the same time as Pope Leo XIII wrote his groundbreaking encyclical in 1891 on social teaching, *Rerum Novarum*.[52] Part of the intellectual backdrop for the encyclical was the work of French social thinkers such as Léon Harmel and Albert de Mun, and these remained influential for Maurin.[53] After leaving the Christian Brothers in 1902 Maurin came under the influence of another important figure in this tradition, Marc Sangnier, the founder of Le Sillon ('the furrow'). This religious movement aimed to re-evangelise the French Republic, organising meetings all over the country to discuss social problems in the light of the Gospel and publishing a journal which at the movement's height had a circulation of 50,000.[54] The movement's enthusiasm for the democratic system (which led to its condemnation) seems to have made Maurin disillusioned with it and he had left it by 1909,[55] when he decided to emigrate to Canada. This seems to have been inspired by a desire to begin again a peasant, subsistence-farming life in a new setting; he was also disillusioned with the religious movements we have mentioned and might also have been trying to avoid military service.

Emigration to Canada and USA

Maurin never returned to France; he went to Canada, to begin a farming life, north of Prince Albert in Saskatchewan.[56] He tried for two years, losing the savings he had sunk into the venture, and then worked for others as a thresher and then on the Canadian pacific railroad. While there he came under the influence of a pacifist – anarchist sect, 'the Christian Community of the Universal Brotherhood', known as the 'Doukabors'. In the years that followed Maurin worked his way into the United States doing a variety of manual jobs and was at one point imprisoned for vagrancy – in Chicago, he worked as a French translator. During all this time, his ideas were developing; as Day herself wrote: 'He read constantly, he worked, he taught. Always he was the teacher. He wrote out his ideas in neat, lettered script, duplicated them, and distributed them himself on street corners, an undignified apostolate.'[57]

Over the years he voraciously read the teachings of the popes and the theologians of the Church, and also came under the influence of the personalist philosopher Emmanuel Mounier, together with other thinkers such as

Tawney, Kropotkin and Tolstoy; he was also immersed in the lives of the saints. His hard labour did give him time for reflection, and he came to see poverty as a gift from God to be embraced and welcomed in a radical manner. What is personalism?

'Personalism was an expression of disdain for political economic structures as they were evolving in the early twentieth century. Specifically, it defined itself as a protest against all philosophies of materialism, including fascism, communism, and bourgeois capitalism. Personalists did not advocate supremacy of the spiritual over the material; rather, they sought to bring these two dimensions of human personality into greater harmony.'[58]

Maurin's thinking

For Maurin, the key way of making this vision real was through the life of the Catholic Church. It was the Church, not the state, which had the *responsibility* for the welfare of the community: it should provide food for the poor and shelter for the homeless. This was a refreshed, new vision of the Gospel, 'in which it would be easier for men to be good.' He further developed these ideas by calling for people to return to small rural, farming communities, which he termed 'agronomic universities', to develop small-scale subsistence farming and respect for the land.

All these ideas involved a rejection of the concept of earning wages or salaries for one's work: there was no shame in begging, in asking for basic support from others, and it demanded showing the same generosity to those in need.[59] So by the time Day met him Maurin lived in this manner, not afraid to ask for help from people he collared in the street, but frequently giving away money, food and clothes to others. In these years he carried out his teaching vocation by talking to strangers, addressing people – usually the poor and the unemployed - in places like Union Square in New York, and handing out pieces of paper, often painstakingly copied by hand, which expounded his teachings. Charity had to be *personal* – it was quite immoral to shift the responsibility to someone else. Day wrote of his beliefs:

'…We are our brother's keeper, and the unit of society is the family… we must have a sense of personal responsibility to take care of our own, and our neighbour, at a personal sacrifice. "That is the first principle," he always said. "It is not the function of the state to enter into these realms. Only in times of great crisis, like floods, hurricane, earthquake or drought, does public authority come in. Charity is personal. Charity is love." He admitted we were in a crisis then, but he wanted none of state relief…'[60]

Maurin's writings were written in a curious mixture of prose and poetry, what he called 'easy essays'. He also liked to coin phrases which he would repeat over and over again, perhaps because English was not his first language – so his vision for new Christian communities was based on what he called 'cult, culture and cultivation': so they had to be rooted in the worship of God, to involve constant education and discussion, and they had to engage with growing things on the land, with manual tasks.[61]

Just as anarchism, as Dorothy had experienced it during and after the First World War, had points of contact with the ways in which small units, close to the people, were commended through the concept of subsidiarity in the social teaching of the Catholic Church, so Maurin's personalism is even more closely rooted in that teaching, taking it to logical conclusions. Pope Pius XI's social encyclical *Quadragesimo Anno* was published in 1931, extolling decision-making and practical support at the closest possible level to those being helped, valuing (as Maurin did) medieval craft guilds; the pope was also deeply concerned, both in this letter and subsequent letters, at the growing and greedy power of the state.[61] Maurin saw all his work as rooted in Catholic theology, the example of the saints and the social teachings of the popes.

The *Catholic Worker* Paper

'..He aroused in you a sense of your own capacities for work, for accomplishment. He made you feel that you and all men had great and generous hearts with which to love God.'[63]

After meeting Dorothy and reading her already published articles it was clear to Maurin what was to happen next:

'....His programme of action: round-table discussions, houses of hospitality and agronomic universities. We were to popularise this program for immediate needs, which in itself would be the seed of a long-range program, a green revolution, by publishing a paper for the man in the street.'[64]

The houses of hospitality were to bring about the practice of the spiritual and corporal works of mercy; the farming communes, especially in the context of the early 1930s, were to remedy the terrible problem of unemployment. We will now look at how the paper and the movement behind it developed from 1933.

The paper

Day was an experienced and passionate journalist and the paper was to be at the centre of the remainder of her life. It was decided to make it a monthly tabloid, of eight pages. Aimed at the 'man in the street', it was to cost only one cent (or 'penny', as a cent is often called in the US), but in practice could often be simply given away. It would be financed by gifts and labour voluntarily given. Very early on it was produced in kitchens and in whatever rooms the writers were in. It was launched on May Day 1933 – Forest begins his biography by describing it being distributed at a massive rally on that day in Union Square.

The paper grew in a spectacular manner. The first print run was 2,500 copies; by the end of the first year the circulation was 100,000 and by 1936 it was 150,000. It caught the imagination of the Catholic community in a way that could not have been predicted, with many parishes and schools taking big bulk orders; but it also reached a much wider readership. Maurin had wanted it called 'The Catholic Radical' but Day's background in the politics of industrial relations determined the title which has prevailed till today, when the original *Catholic Worker* paper in New York has been joined by similar papers in other American cities and elsewhere in the world.

There were tensions at the beginning. Maurin gave the impression that he simply wanted it to be a vehicle for his own thoughts. While these remained a mainstay until he died and indeed after his death, (the 'easy essays' appear in issues today) the process of applying the social teachings of the Church to everyday life required a broader approach. Day was far more interested than he was in industrial disputes ('strikes don't strike me', he would say, because of his questioning of the wage system and modern industry), so these received a lot of coverage and committed support. As we shall examine in more detail, the paper was also resolutely committed to peace and non-violence. The paper inspired many young people and others who gave of their time and whose lives became centred on it: Day describes many colourful characters who helped in the production and distribution.

Houses of hospitality

Day makes it clear that the vision of 'houses of hospitality' actually began to take root simply around the practicalities of getting a newspaper produced. People weren't paid salaries at the paper to do so was foreign to its philosophy (and in any case there was no money), so it made sense to feed and house those who were helping to get the paper out. This was another part of Maurin's vision, rooted in what he saw of the practice of the early Church, which grew very quickly, so that by the outbreak of the Second World War there were Catholic Worker houses of hospitality in virtually every American city. This was not simply because the idea caught people's imagination: it was because of real social need, the terrible poverty of the Depression years. The houses also got volunteers from men coming out of college without jobs who had read the paper as students. So the 'bread line', which fed (for example) with bread and soup hundreds each day in Mott Street in the Lower East Side of New York, was fundamental to the mission of the *Catholic Worker* – simply showing the love of Christ to those in need, unconditionally and without calculation. They fed all those who came for food and drink; people who stayed were not asked to leave. A great deal of hardship was experienced as Day explains:

> 'Voluntary poverty means a good deal of discomfort in these houses of ours, Many of the houses throughout the country are without central heating and have to be warmed by stoves in winter. There are back-yard toilets for some even now. [1952] The first Philadelphia house had to use water drawn from one spigot at the end of an alley, which serves half a dozen other houses. It was lit with oil lamps. It was cold and damp and so unbelievably poverty-stricken that little children coming to see who were the young people meeting there exclaimed that this

could not be a *Catholic* place: it was too poor. We must be Communists…'[65]

Faith centred

The practice of the faith was central to the life of the houses. Churches were not far away and Day, Maurin and others were able to go to Mass every day; in time chapels were constructed within houses. Many priests gave up their vacations to come and give retreats and days of recollection, such as Father Pacifique Roy[66] and Father John Hugo. The practical work of charity carried out through the houses earned the movement a great deal of respect from the authorities of the Church; even when bishops felt challenged by parts of the radical message of the paper, they still gave it financial support. The growing confidence and wealth of the Catholic Church in America made it a fertile ground for a new and exciting movement; but as some commentators have pointed out the *Catholic Worker* did not fit neatly into the growing social activism of the American Church, and it certainly did not line up behind those in the Church who welcomed President Roosevelt's 'New Deal'.[67]

The commitment of the paper and the movement to workers on strike sometimes brought about direct conflict with the authorities of the Church, as in the strike by gravediggers in the New York diocesan cemetery in 1949.[68]

Against usury

Another distinctive feature of the paper and the communities inspired by it was a resistance to usury, based on Maurin's study of classic medieval theologians. For him, acceptance of usury was a bad fruit of Calvin's reforms in the 16th century which had led the Catholic Church astray. In 1960 Day returned to the New York City Treasurer a cheque for $3,579.39, which was interest on a property which had been appropriated. Day wrote these words which have a particular resonance in our own day:

> 'We are returning the interest on the money we have recently received because we do not believe in "money lending" at interest. As Catholics we are acquainted with the early teaching of the Church. All the early councils forbade it, declaring it reprehensible to make money by lending it out at interest. Canon law of the Middle Ages forbade it and in various dioceses ordered that profit so obtained was to be restored. In the Christian emphasis on the duty of charity, even in the case of confiscation, as in our own case – not to resist but to accept cheerfully.

> We do not believe in the profit system, and so we cannot take profit or interest on our money.... Loaning money at interest is deemed by one

Franciscan as the principal scourge of civilisation. Eric Gill, the English artist and writer, calls usury and war the two great problems of our time.'[69]

Agronomic universities

The third part of Maurin's vision was, in the long term, the least successful, but it remains integral today to what the movement is about: in many ways it was the part that was closer to his heart, more than the other things which were more dramatically achieved. Maurin began writing about the need to live out his vision in farming communities in 1935, and the first Catholic Worker farm, at Easton in Pennsylvania, was bought in May 1936. In the initial years farms sprung up in many parts of the country (New Jersey, Massachusetts, Ohio, Michigan) and, again, the idea caught people's imagination. The farms were not 'commercial': they aimed at providing for the needs of the families and others there, and practised a gentle form of agriculture, reviving the medieval custom of gleaning the fields. Maurin believed that the mass commercialisation of agriculture in the United States after the Civil War had been mistaken.[70] His critique of the effects of the capitalist system on farming was supported by the theologian Fr John Hugo.

Like the houses of hospitality, the farms were centred on the practice of the faith, and chapels were built from wood and other local materials; some became retreat centres.[71] There was also an affectionate attitude towards the animals on the farms, often given names. While the farms have always remained a big part of the Catholic Worker movement, and in our own age show a prophetic respect for the environment more recognised than it was seventy years ago (they pioneered the use of organic fertilisers), the number of farms has not been great and after the initial years many failed and were closed. A big problem was simply 'staying power' on the part of volunteers, and the simple inability of many to work hard enough – early mornings, long hours, very hard physical work; in addition people were in the communities with different agendas. Day wrote:

> 'Some were started and abandoned as too isolated, or because of lack of water, lack of funds, lack of people who knew how to work....the family thought Peter's farming commune was solely for them. The scholars thought the agronomic university idea was for them. The sick and unemployed thought the Catholic Worker farms in general were for women and children and the helpless.'[72]

Vision for Peace

Just after the outbreak of the Second World War Day
wrote:

> 'St Augustine says that we are all members or
> potential members of the mystical Body of Christ.
> Therefore all men are our neighbours and Christ
> told us we should love our neighbours, whether they
> be friend or enemy.'[73]

This understanding of the doctrine of the Mystical
Body of Christ was the basis of Day's pacifism, her
opposition to all forms of war – simple and
straightforward, perhaps too much for many people. Love
of neighbour simply forbids Christians from taking up
arms against others, whatever the circumstances.[74] By the
time the Second World War broke out and the USA
entered it in 1941, the pacifist position of Day and the
Catholic Worker movement had already been
controversial within the Catholic community. The
movement was opposed to the Italian invasion of
Abyssinia in 1935 which enjoyed support from the
Catholic Church in Italy; far more controversially, it
opposed involvement on one side or the other in the

Spanish Civil War from 1936. Many Catholics, including hundreds of priests and religious, were killed by Republican forces before and during the conflict, and countless churches destroyed; except in the Basque country, the Church was clearly allied to General Franco and the Nationalists. Day's refusal to support him cost the *Catholic Worker* many subscribers and the support of a number of American bishops.[75] Day was not endorsing in any way those whom she thought should not be opposed by military force: the movement early on supported victims of the Nazis and also picketed in 1934 the Mexican consulate in New York, a very large demonstration included many school students, as a result of the anti-Catholic persecution there.[76]

It is quite wrong for this absolute pacifism to be shown as something easy, sentimental or a 'soft option'. As Thomas Merton, one of the great prophets of Catholic teaching about peace in the twentieth century, pointed out in reference to Day:

> 'There are many reasons to believe that the social action of someone like Dorothy Day, who is willing to refuse cooperation even in civil defense drills and ready to go to jail for her belief in peace, is far more significantly Christian than the rather subtle and comfy positions of certain casuists. When I consider that Dorothy Day was confined to a jail cell in

nothing but a light wrap (her clothes having been taken from her) and that she could only get to Mass and Communion in the prison by dressing in clothes borrowed from prostitutes and thieves in the neighbouring cells, then I lose all inclination to take seriously the self-complacent nonsense of those who consider her kind of pacifism sentimental.'[77]

World War II

When the US entered the Second World War Day's opposition, based on her absolute pacifism, caused controversy and division within the movement. Many houses of hospitality closed and bread lines shortened because men were drafted or given employment as part of the war effort. She wrote:

'Dear fellow workers in Christ: Lord God, merciful God, our Father, shall we keep silent, or shall we speak?... We will print the words of Christ, who is with us always, even to the end of the world. "Love your enemies, do good to those who hate you, and pray for those who persecute and calumniate you, so that you may be children of your Father in heaven, who makes His sun to rise on the good and the evil, and sends rain on the just and the unjust"...We are still pacifists. Our manifesto is the Sermon on the Mount, which means that we will try to be peacemakers. Speaking for many of our conscientious objectors, we will not participate in armed warfare or in making munitions, or by buying government bonds to prosecute the war, or in urging others to these efforts.

But neither will we be carping in our criticism. We love our country and we love our President. We have been the only country in the world where men and women of all nations have taken refuge from oppression. We recognise that while in the order of intention we have tried to stand for peace, for love of our brothers and sisters, in the order of execution we have failed as Americans in living up to our principles. We will try daily, hourly, to pray for an end to the war....'[78]

Many years later the Second Vatican Council, in its Pastoral Council on the Church in the Modern World, *Gaudium et Spes*, affirmed the right to conscientious objection. Many who object to most modern wars, and welcome the Church's growing opposition to war, would nevertheless assert that military action against the Nazis was justified; however it is incumbent on all Catholics to respect and understand the position of absolute pacifists like Day.

Hiroshima and Nagasaki

From the end of the Second World War the work for peace
by Day and countless others was focussed on the means by
which the war ended – the dropping of the first atomic
bombs on Japan and the build-up in nuclear weapons
which followed. As for many other Catholics of varying
backgrounds all over the world,[79] the bombing of
Hiroshima and Nagasaki was a horrifying event for Day.
There is greater passion than usual in these words:

'Mr Truman was jubilant. President Truman. True
man; what a strange name, come to think of it. We
refer to Jesus Christ as true God and true Man.
Truman is a true man of his time in that he was
jubilant. He was not a son of God, brother of
Christ, brother of the Japanese, jubilating as he did.
He went from table to table on the cruiser which
was bringing him home from the Big Three
conference, telling the great news; "jubilant" the
newspapers said. *Jubilate Deo*. We have killed
318,000 Japanese.

That is, we hope we have killed them, the
Associated Press, on page one, column one, of the
Herald Tribune says. The effect is hoped for, not
known. It is to be hoped they are vaporized, our
Japanese brothers, scattered, men, women, and

babies, to the four winds, over the seven seas. Perhaps we will breathe their dust into our nostrils, feel them in the fog of New York in our faces, feel them in the rain on the hills of Easton. *Jubilate Deo*. President Truman was jubilant. We have created. We have created destruction. We have created a new element, called Pluto. Nature has nothing to do with it.

"A cavern below Columbia was the bomb's cradle," born not that men might live, but that men might be killed. Brought into being in a cavern, and then tried in a desert place, in the midst of tempest and lightning, tried out, and then again on the eve of the Feast of the Transfiguration of Our Lord Jesus Christ, on a far-off island in the Eastern Hemisphere, tried out again, this "new weapon which conceivably might wipe out mankind, and perhaps the planet itself"... ...Scientists, army officers, great universities (Notre Dame included), and captains of industry – all are given credit lines in the press for their work of preparing the bomb – and other bombs, the President assures us, are in production now.

Great Britain controls the supply of uranium ore in Canada and Rhodesia. We are making the bombs. This great new force will be used for good, the scientists tell us. And then they wiped out a city of 318,000. This was good. The President was jubilant... ...God is still in the picture. God is not mocked.... We are held in God's hands, all of us, and President Truman too, and these scientists who have created death, but will use it for good. He, God, holds our life and our happiness, our sanity and our health; our lives are in His hands. He is our creator. Creator...'[80]

These were not easy times: on 15 May 1949, after some years of debilitation, Peter Maurin died peacefully at the farm in Easton. He was buried in Queens, New York.[81]

Opposition to nuclear weapons

In the bleak years of the Cold War that followed, the Catholic Worker movement manifested its opposition to nuclear weapons by refusing to take part in civil defence drills in New York. For Day such drills perpetuated the lie that a nuclear war would be something people could survive and win. For example, on 15 June 1955 Day and others, during a drill, sat down in front of City Hall, an act of disobedience which was also a penance for the dropping of the atomic bombs on Japan. As a Catholic Worker leaflet explained:

'In the name of Jesus, who is God, who is Love, we will not obey this order to pretend, to evacuate, to hide. We will not be drilled into fear. We do not have faith in God if we depend upon the Atom bomb.'

Year by year Day and others were imprisoned for this act, but more and more people came out to demonstrate against the drill – by 1961 2,000 were doing so, and the drill was never put on again. During these years few Catholics in the western world supported the opposition of the Catholic Worker movement to nuclear weapons and the international policies based on the intention to use them. Indeed, in the United States clergy such as Thomas Merton were often prevented by their superiors from writing about the issue – the Catholic challenge to nuclear weapons was led by laypeople.[82] This began to change with the pontificate of Blessed John XXIII: in 1963 Day went to Rome with a group of 'Mothers for Peace' to thank the pope for the encyclical Pacem in Terris. This letter significantly shifted Catholic teaching towards an outright condemnation of war.[83] The pope was too ill for a private audience, but gave them a blessing and asked them to continue in what they were doing. Another action of civil disobedience which both individuals and the newspaper itself took was the withholding of federal (as opposed to State) taxes as these financed the American war machine. By the 1970s this had almost led to punitive fines and closure, but in the end a compromise was reached.[84]

Vatican Council II: vindication

This shift was also evident in the proceedings of the Second Vatican Council. As the council was ending, in late 1965, Day went to Rome to fast, expressing the hope that the Council fathers would issue 'a clear statement, "Put away thy sword."' The council's final document, its Pastoral Constitution on the Church in the Modern World, *Gaudium et Spes*, roundly condemned indiscriminate acts of war against the innocent, called for legal protection for conscientious objectors and described as 'criminal' those who obey commands to kill the innocent and defenceless.[85] Thus were Day and the Catholic Worker Movement vindicated, after years of abuse and vilification.

The Vietnam War and the intensive bombing of Vietnam, Laos and Cambodia by the Americans provided a good example of what the Council was condemning – indeed, Pope Paul VI clashed openly with President Lyndon Johnson over the war.[86] Day, alongside the Cistercian Thomas Merton and the Berrigan brothers, was at the forefront of Catholic opposition to the war, with many in the Catholic Worker movement being imprisoned for resisting conscription. She was one of a small group which founded the group PAX, which later became Pax Christi, now the worldwide Catholic peace organisation. Annual PAX conferences were held from 1964 to 1970 at the Catholic Worker farm at Tivoli, New York state.

As the Church worldwide received and took to its heart the teachings of the Council, and as a result too of the witness for peace and justice shown by Pope Paul VI in his 1967 encyclical *Populorum Progressio*[87] and in other ways, Dorothy saw her work vindicated in affirmed in many ways, at least within the Church. She was not afraid to criticise those who were slow to realise how Christian teaching about peace was shifting, for example her own Ordinary, the Archbishop of New York:

> 'I have often thought it is a brave thing to do, these Christmas visits of Cardinal Spellman to the American troops all over the world, Europe, Korea, Vietnam. But oh, God, what are all these Americans, so-called Christians, doing all over the world so far from their own shores?

> But what words are those he spoke – going against even the Pope, calling for victory, total victory? Words are as strong and powerful as bombs, as napalm. How much the government counts on these words, pays for those words to exalt our own way of life, to build up fear of the enemy. Deliver us, Lord, from the fear of the enemy. That is one of the lines in the Psalms, and we are not asking God to deliver us from enemies but from the fear of them. Love casts out fear, but we have to get over the fear in order to get close enough to love them.'[88]

Also in 1967, she travelled to Rome for the International Congress of the Laity and received Holy Communion from the hands of Pope Paul VI. Another part of the movement's witness to peace, and their spirit of openness towards countries which were moving away from the capitalist system, was her positive attitude towards Cuba after the revolution of Fidel Castro, which she visited in 1962, at the height of tension between Cuba and the USA.[89] Also during these years Day and the movement campaigned vigorously on behalf of those facing execution in American prisons, and for Civil Rights – Day went to the South to show her support for the *Koinonia* farm in Georgia[90] which had been attacked by the Ku Klux Klan, and the car she was in was shot at.

Closing Years and Death

In the last ten years of her life Dorothy's health declined –
in 1970 she was diagnosed with an enlarged heart, water
in the lungs and hardened arteries. This did not slow her
down very much: she went on visits to Russia, Eastern
Europe and India, where she met Blessed Mother Teresa
of Calcutta: she spoke to her novice sisters about going to
prison for the sake of the gospels. Mother Teresa pinned
on Dorothy's dress the cross worn only by professed
members of the Missionary Sisters of Charity.

Imprisonment again

In 1973 she took part in a demonstration (together with
nearly a hundred priests and nuns) in Fresno, California, in
support of the United Farm workers, led by Cesar Chavez.
She felt the UFW was an important social and religious
movement, more so than most American Trade Unions.
Thousands of striking and picketing farm workers (some
of them Muslim Arabs) were jailed that summer – the
UFW was betrayed by one of the country's largest and
most powerful unions, the Teamsters, whose members
broke the strike and took over the strikers' work.

Day had come to California for a conference organised
by Joan Baez, but instead she was arrested and

imprisoned (for the last time) for ten days. Shortly afterwards she wrote:

'The strike was widespread and mass arrests were continuing. My path was clear: the U.F.W. has everything that belongs to a new social order. Since I had come to picket where an injunction was prohibiting picketing, it appeared that I would spend my weeks in California in jail, not at conferences... I must mention a prayer I wrote in the front of my New Testament, and hope our readers, while they read, say this for the strikers.

Dear Pope John – please, yourself a *campesino*, watch over the United Farm Workers. Raise up more and more leader-servants throughout the country to stand with Cesar Chavez in this non-violent struggle with Mammon, in all the rural districts of North and South, in the cotton fields, beet fields, potato fields, in our orchards and vineyards, our orange groves – wherever men, women, and children work on the land. Help make a new order wherein justice flourishes, and, as Peter Maurin, himself a peasant, said so simply, "where it is easier to be good."[91]

During these years she was distressed by the decline in religious practice and people leaving the priesthood and religious life; she continued to use the pre-conciliar

Breviary.[92] On 6 August 1976 she spoke at the Eucharistic Congress in Philadelphia. She spoke about her love of God, about how we need to take that love into all creation, and about the Church. She pointed out that it was Hiroshima Day and that such acts of destruction directly opposed God who 'gave us life, and the Eucharist to sustain our life.'[93]

Last years

The following month she had a heart attack. Although physically frail and no longer able to travel - she told those who replied to invitations she received to say 'Tell them I'm in a state of nervous decline' - she continued writing, though less often.[94] At this time she was visited by Blessed Mother Teresa. She died in the early evening of 29 November 1980, with her daughter Tamar Teresa at her side. Her funeral was at Nativity Church in New York, attended by hundreds of people and celebrated by Cardinal Terence Cooke, the Archbishop of New York, and she was buried in a meadow on Staten Island overlooking the ocean, the place where she had been living when her daughter had been born and she had decided to become a Catholic. Her simple gravestone bears a loaves and fishes motif and the words

DOROTHY DAY

NOVEMBER 8, 1897 – NOVEMBER 29, 1980

DEO GRATIAS

Her Holiness and Theology

'We are all called to be saints, and we might as well get over our bourgeois fear of the name. We might also get used to recognising that there is some of the saint in all of us. Inasmuch as we are growing, putting off the old man and putting on Christ, there is some of the saint, the body, the divine right there.'[95]

What we have seen of Dorothy Day's life has shown how she lived her Christian life with a growing sense of closeness to God and faithfulness to the teachings of Christ. It is her holiness and her teachings which give her abiding importance for the whole Church. We can look at this holiness under four headings

Love of God, love of the poor

The heart of the message of Day, Maurin and the *Catholic Worker* is the boundless love of God for humanity, which we are called as Christ's baptised followers to share with others, particularly the poor. In the poor we simply encounter Christ and meet him. The exuberance of this sense of love is captured in this passage:

'We want to be happy, we want others to be happy, we want to see some of this joy of life which children haven, we want to see people intoxicated with God, or just filled with the good steady joy of knowing that Christ is King and that we are His flock and He has prepared for us a kingdom, and that God loves us as a father lives his children, as a bridegroom loves his bride, and that eye hath not seen nor ear heard what God hath prepared for us!'[96]

It was this love which made, and still makes, the charitable work of the *Catholic Worker* communities so distinctive and challenging. Quoting St Catherine of Siena,[97] she castigated those who distinguished between the 'deserving' and 'undeserving' poor. This boundlessness, which meant that there was never enough money around to keep the work going, also set the movement apart from more conventional charitable work carried out in the name of the Church.[98] It is quite wrong, however, to see this as sentimental or not 'thought through'; by contrast, as the fruit of much 'clarification of thought' around kitchen tables with Peter Maurin, it is systematically presented in her writings. Day addresses the four classic 'dimensions of love' – God's love for us, our love for him, our love for each other, and our self-love.[99] Her love for the poor was wholly Christocentric:

'Let us rejoice in poverty, because Christ was poor. Let us love to live with the poor, because they are specially loved by Christ. Even the lowest, most depraved, we must see Christ in them, and love them to folly. When we suffer from dirt, lack of privacy, heat and cold, coarse food, let us rejoice.'[100]

The Mass and the other sacraments

For Day, as for all Catholics, God's love for us is mediated through the sacraments of the Church, the use God makes of material things to impart his grace. We saw above how long before she became a Catholic, she was fascinated by the experience of the Mass, even though she did not know what was going on. Her faith in the Mass, in the miracle of transubstantiation, made the doctrine of the Incarnation more real, as she shows in this passage:

'It is because we forget the humanity of Christ – present with us today in the Blessed Sacrament just as truly as when He walked with His apostles through the cornfields that Sunday long ago, breakfasting on the ears of corn – that we have ignored the material claims of our fellow man during this capitalistic, industrialist era…'[101]

She wrote of the awesomeness of receiving Holy Communion daily; in her last years it is recorded that when she was brought Communion in her room, she would prepare for an hour beforehand, and give thanks for an hour afterwards. This is her beautiful picture of praying before the Blessed Sacrament:

'If the heart is clear, a warm sunshiny day brings joy and health to the body. We do not think of the sun, we feel the warmth of the sun all about us, we feel it in the air, we see it reflected in people's faces, we can feel buds bursting on the tress in the parks. It is like that to sit in the presence of the Blessed Sacrament in church. We do nothing, we don't think, or we have distractions, perhaps. The memory and understanding are feeble, but our good will has brought us there – our will to love and to be loved. Christ there in the tabernacle, in His humanity and divinity, is like the sun acting upon us, healing us of our infirmities. We bathe ourselves in this sunlight which warms and heals us. *Lord, take away my heart of stone and give me a heart of flesh*, a warm heart that beats with thy love.'[102]

Like many converts reared on this experience of the Mass, Day was a little sceptical about liturgical reforms and unimpressed by some excesses in the 1960s.[103] Her consciousness of God's action through the sacraments is shown in other ways too, such as her experience of God's forgiveness in confession (and she deplored the decline in the practice of confession from the 1960s) and there are many accounts in her writings of members of the Catholic Worker family being anointed before death. For her the sacraments were never (as they are for some) a means of escaping from the world and its sufferings: rather they were the means through which God meets us day by day with his healing grace.

The Saints

Even before she became a Catholic, Dorothy experienced a great closeness to the saints: 'When I worked about the house, I found myself addressing the Blessed Virgin and turning toward her statue.'[104] Part of her reading at this time was a life of St Teresa of Avila: from the very beginning of her life as a Catholic Dorothy saw the saints as her friends within the Church. Her closeness to Our Lady is very natural and striking, rooted in everyday life:

'This morning, after Communion, I thought of writing about Mary, and since the thought came to me at *that* time, I took it as an order. I always say to the Blessed Mother after Communion – "Here He is in my heart; I believe, help thou my unbelief; Adore Him, thank Him and love Him for me. He is your Son; His honour is in your hands. Do not let me dishonour Him."

And since, too, at that moment came this thought, those glimpses of all she has meant to me – all the little contacts with her that brought me to Him – I felt I must write.

One of the reasons I do not write more is that there is always housework, cleaning, scrubbing, sewing, washing (right now it is cleaning fish), etc., to do. Just as she had to do these things, and probably never neglected them. But then, too, I can see her sitting seemingly idle beside a well on just such a day as this, just thanking Him, with each happy breath…

When my daughter was born almost eighteen years ago, I turned her over to the Blessed Mother. "What kind of a mother am I going to be?" I kept thinking to myself… There was a solution, of course, to such a difficulty. "You," I told the Blessed Mother, "will have to be her mother. Under the best of circumstances I'm a failure as a homemaker. I'm untidy, inconsistent, undisciplined, temperamental, and I have to pray every day for final perseverance…." It is only in these last few years that it has occurred to me why my daughter has never called me "Mother." From the time she first spoke, it was "Dorothy"…. It came like a flash of light. "The Blessed Virgin Mary is Mother of my child. No harm can ever come to her with such a Mother."' [105]

When Dorothy was being 'indoctrinated' by Peter Maurin, he taught her a great deal about the lives of the saints, and her writings after are full of reflections about them, including saints who would normally be considered obscure, such as St Apollo, St Thalaleus or St Baldmerus. All the saints and their lives had a message: we are called to be holy; we can all be saints like them.

One who made a particular impression on her was the Little Flower, St Thérèse of Lisieux, of whom she wrote a biography.[106] Her interest in her went back to her time in a maternity hospital before the birth of her daughter, when the girl in the next bed gave her a medal of St Thérèse. She was not initially attracted to her; the fascination came gradually. Day reflects that given her background, Thérèse would have been an unlikely left-wing agitator[107]; what appealed to her was her simplicity and her life centred on love for God: "Oh I love Him. My God, I love you!"

> These were her last words. The sisters were summoned quickly back into the infirmary to kneel about the bedside and to witness the last moments of this girl who wished to die of love... ...it was the "worker", the common man, who first spread her fame by word of mouth. It was the masses who first proclaimed her a saint. It was the "people".

What was there about her to make such an appeal? Perhaps because she was so much like the rest of us in her ordinariness. In her lifetime there are no miracles recounted; she was just good, good as the bread which the Normans bake in huge loaves. Good as the pale cider which takes the place of the wine of the rest of France, since Normandy is an apple country.'[108]

For Day, the saints are our friends and fellow workers, Catholic workers.

'A very erratic and irresponsible person'

Jesus tells us in the Sermon on the Mount that we are blessed and happy when we are reviled and abused for his sake. A consistent mark of holiness, of the saint, is being able so to suffer. Just as St Thérèse longed to suffer martyrdom, so Dorothy was always aware that faithfulness the gospel entailed hardship and persecution: she had, in a sense, anticipated this before her conversion in her witness for the poor and the oppressed. Like many conversions, her embrace of Christianity in 1927 did not entail a complete turning away from her convictions: rather, they were fulfilled and given new meaning. The love for the poor she had felt from an early age and pursued as a young radical, the ally of communists,[109] was given greater authenticity by her Catholic faith and by her vision for the Catholic Church. This was and remained deeply threatening to the rich and the powerful in American society, and was unsettling to many in the Church as well: in the 1950s the paper was banned in the Westminster diocese by Cardinal Bernard Griffin for being 'communist'.[110] The Catholic Worker movement's espousal of non-violent resistance, of support for striking workers and other oppressed people, frequently brought it into conflict with the powers of the state, at a time in America of great fear of Communism. She was arrested and imprisoned no less often after she became a Catholic, right up until seven years before her death. Many of her positions alienated some within the Church; they also meant that the powerful saw her as a dangerous subversive. The infamous J. Edgar Hoover, Head of the FBI, three times attempted to put her on trial for sedition, unsuccessfully. This is what he wrote about her in her 500-page FBI dossier:

'Dorothy Day has been described as a very erratic and irresponsible person...She maintains a very hostile and belligerent attitude toward the Bureau and makes every effort to castigate the Bureau whenever she feels so inclined.'[111]

This characteristic, of resistance to the power of the state, is the final mark of holiness which we can identify. Throughout the history of the Church, and perhaps particularly the twentieth century, this has defined Christian witness, particularly in the lives of the martyrs, men and women like Blessed Franz Jägerstätter, St Teresa Benedicta of the Cross, the Servant of God Oscar Romero and countless others. The hardships Dorothy Day endured in the name of witness for the poor and resistance to the false message of war, place her firmly in that tradition of holiness. The likes of Hoover were right to feel threatened.

All the characteristics of Dorothy Day's life enable us to see her as a great and holy Christian witness for our age. Some of the causes she served have been advanced: the Catholic Church as an institution has officially embraced the 'preferential option for the poor'; the Church is also now a consistent witness for peace, and constantly challenges the dark forces of militarism, in Europe and the United States. But there is still a gulf between what Day and Maurin taught and where Catholics are: first, there is still on the part of many Catholics an uncritical and easy-going view of the power of the state (although this is far from Church teaching); it is also true that because the numerical 'heartlands' of the Church, both in the USA and in western Europe, are now in affluent rather than poor areas (compared to the 1930s) many Catholics, in spite of papal teachings, are still at ease with the free-market, capitalist world view and can be very resistant to even mild campaigning for peace and social justice in the name of the Church; finally, the Church is a long way from returning to the traditional Christian condemnation of usury.

Above all the *method* by which Day sought to show Christ's love remains a big challenge. The Church is, if anything, even less critical of state-provided welfare than it was seventy years ago. We do not have, as Maurin wanted, a house of hospitality in every parish. Indeed, direct charitable activity for the poor by the churches is in some respects more threatened by state power than in the past (as in the case of Catholic adoption agencies in this country), partly because of lack of money – an excuse, of course, which would not have satisfied Day or Maurin.

Day wrote of those who came into contact with Maurin that 'though they themselves fail to go the whole way, their faces are turned at least toward the light.' She would never be satisfied with that, of course, but those words do help us understand how great her influence has been, and how much more it can achieve as we learn more of her life and listen to her words.

The *Catholic Worker* Movement Today

Gamaliel's words, 'If this enterprise, this movement of theirs, is of human origin, it will break up of its own accord'[112] are worth applying to the paper and the movement Dorothy Day founded. The *Catholic Worker* paper still appears in its original form in New York, and there are sister papers in other American cities, Australia and England. There are also Catholic Worker communities in Belgium, Canada, Germany, Mexico, New Zealand, and many of these produce newsletters. The aims of the movement remain true to Day's vision:

'The aim of the Catholic Worker movement is to live in accordance with the justice and charity of Jesus Christ. Our sources are the Hebrew and Greek Scriptures as handed down in the teachings of the Roman Catholic Church, with our inspiration coming from the lives of the saints, "men and women outstanding in holiness, living witnesses to Your unchanging love."[113]

The oldest community in England is St Francis House in east Oxford. It offers hospitality to asylum seekers, runs an organic garden and is involved in resistance to war and publishes a newsletter.[114]

The Catholic Worker house in London is Dorothy Day House in Hackney.

'Our vision is of a faith based community of hospitality and resistance: "in house", we provide accommodation for "destitute refugees"...Our outreach work consists of running Peter's Community Café and the Urban Table soup kitchen...during Advent we vigilled weekly outside the Home Office reporting and detention centre at Old Street....this week we start an anti-war-on-terror vigil on the high street in Dalston.'[115]

The Catholic Worker Farm in West Hyde, Hertfordshire, established in August 2006, is also a house of hospitality:

'We offer hospitality to those who need help. Presently we host 6 marginalised people. These women need advocacy, accompaniment and emotional support. Living on a farm has given us the opportunity to become as self-sufficient as possible, growing organic fruit and vegetables in the permaculture style and hoping one day to have chickens...'[116]

People from the farm also carry out vigils at the Northwood Joint Forces Military HQ, the nerve centre for British war efforts.

The *London Catholic Worker*[117] and other material shows how faithful the movement remains to the vision of Day and Maurin: living in voluntary poverty, offering practical help to the most vulnerable people in this country, and non-violent witness against war and militarism – all grounded in the Catholic faith. If, on the basis of what you have read in this booklet about Dorothy Day, you wish to make a donation for the work of Catholic Worker communities in this country, you can send it to 14 Deal Street, London E1 5AH.

The philosophy of Day and the *Catholic Worker* has been influential on other groups. A good example would be the *Simon Community*, set up in London by Anton Wallich-Clifford, a Catholic, in 1963 to offer support to the 'street homeless'.[118]

Prayer for Dorothy Day's Canonisation

God our creator,
Your servant Dorothy Day exemplified the
Catholic faith by her conversion, life of prayer
and voluntary poverty, works of mercy and
witness to the justice and peace of the Gospel.
May her life inspire people to turn to Christ as
their saviour and guide
To see his face in the world's poor
And to raise their voices for the justice of
God's kingdom.
We pray that your grant the favours we ask
through her intercession
So that her goodness and kindness may be
more widely recognised and one day the
Church may proclaim her saint
We ask this through Christ our Lord

Composed by Mgr Kevin Sullivan, Archdiocese of New York. For details
of the cause see *www.dorothydayguild.org*. Details of favours received
should through the intercession of the Servant of God Dorothy Day be
sent to the Guild for Dorothy Day, Archdiocese of New York, 1011 First
Avenue 12th floor, New York, NY 10022.

Further reading

What follows is only a small selection of published material. Some of the better known books have been republished in Britain. *www.catholicworker.org/search/bibliogeneral.cfm* provides a thorough initial list. Day's archives are at Marquette University library, *www.marquette.edu/library*.

Day, Dorothy

- *The Eleventh Virgin* Albert and Charles Boni, 1924. This is her autobiographical novel (difficult to obtain) which deals with painful episodes in her early life avoided in her other writings: she came to hate it. No film was ever made of it.
- *The Long Loneliness* New York: Harper and Rowe, 1997 (originally published in 1952)
- *Loaves and Fishes* New York: Harper and Rowe, 1963
- *On Pilgrimage* Grand Rapids: Eerdmans, 1999
- *On Pilgrimage: The Sixties*, 1972
- *Thérèse* Springfield: Templegate, 1979
- *Selected Writings*, ed. and intro. Robert Ellsberg London: Darton, Longman and Todd, 2005
- *From Union Square to Rome* Silver Spring: Preservation of the Faith Press, 1938 (the copy in the British Library in London is signed by Day, as she gave it as a Christmas present. The note from the library in the book referring to this describes her as 'the famous liberal Catholic author.' One wonders how she would have reacted to such a description)
- with Francis J. Sicius *Peter Maurin Apostle to the World* Maryknoll: Orbis, 2004

Maurin, Peter *Easy Essays* Chicago: Franciscan Herald, 1984

Scott, David (ed.) *Praying in the Presence of Our Lord with Dorothy Day* Huntingdon: Our Sunday Visitor, 2002

Ellis, Marc *A Year at the Catholic Worker New York*: Paulist Press, 1978

Piehl, M. *Breaking Bread: The Catholic Worker and the Origin of Catholic Radicalism in America* Philadelphia: Temple University Press 1982. This important study looks at the CW movement in the overall context of American Catholicism.

Miller, W. *A Harsh and Dreadful Love: Dorothy Day and the Catholic Worker Movement* New York: Liveright, 1973

Miller, W. *Dorothy Day: A Biography* San Francisco: Harper & Row 1982. This is the most comprehensive and detailed biography, the nearest that there is to an 'official' one. Miller was given Day's private journals.

O'Connor, June *The Moral Vision of Dorothy Day: A Feminist Perspective* New York: Crossroad, 1991

Chittister, Joan, OSB 'Dorothy Day Icon of the Streets' in *A Passion for Life Fragments of the Face of God* Maryknoll: Orbis, 1996, pp. 59ff.

Forest, Jim *Love is the Measure: A Biography of Dorothy Day* Basingstoke: Marshall Pickering, 1987.

O'Shea Merriman, Brigid *Searching for Christ: The Spirituality of Dorothy Day* Notre Dame

Thorn, W., Runkel, P. and Mountin, S. *Dorothy Day and the Catholic Worker* Centenary essays Marquette University Press, 2001

Sheehan, Arthur *Peter Maurin Gay Believer* Garden City: Doubleday, 1959

Scott, David and Aquilina, Mike (eds.) *Weapons of the Spirit: Selected Writings of Father John Hugo* Huntingdon: Our Sunday Visitor

Merton, Thomas *Passion for Peace* ed. William H. Shannon New York: Crossroad, 1996. Nine of the chapters in this collection of Merton's most important writings on peace and social issues originally appeared in the *Catholic Worker*.

Walters, Hugh '*Pro Foco Non Foro* The Thomistic Inheritance and the Household Economy of Father Vincent McNabb' in John Orme Mills OP (ed.) *Justice, Peace, and Dominicans* 1216-2001, Dublin: Dominican Publications, 2001. This article shows the wider influence of Maurin and Day.

Bozza, Mary Louise *Dorothy Day: On Love for God, Neighbor and Self* Unpublished dissertation, available online: *dissertations.bc.edu/cgi/viewcontent.cgi?article=1002&context=ashonors*

Online database: The Dorothy Day Library: *http://www.catholicworker.org/dorothyday/index.cfm* for Day's writings, together with much related material. The New York *Catholic Worker* itself is not available online. It is still published monthly, for 1 US cent, from 36 E. First Street, New York, NY 10003. See also the *Houston Catholic Worker*, P.O. Box 70113, Houston, TX 77270, *www.cjd.org*. For Catholic Worker communities in London and Hertfordshire, *www.londoncatholicworker.org*. Booklets from Pax Christi USA, *www.paxchristiusa.org*. There is also a Catholic Worker paper and movement in Australia.[119]

Films: *Entertaining Angels*, directed by Michael Ray Rhodes, starring Moira Kelly as Dorothy Day and Martin Sheen as Peter Maurin, Paulist Pictures, 1996. *Dorothy Day: Don't Call me a Saint*, written, directed and produced by Claudia Larson, available from *http://dorothydaydoc.com/home.html*. *Fool for Christ*, written and made by Sarah Melici. The London Catholic Worker community, 14 Deal St, London E1 5AH; email *londoncatholicworker@yahoo.co.uk* to order the DVD.

Endnotes

[1] David Scott, *Praying in the Presence of Our Lord with Dorothy Day* (Huntingdon: Our Sunday Visitor 2002), endpiece.

[2] See the instruction of the Sacred Congregation for the Doctrine of the Faith, *Libertatis Conscientia* (1986) section 68, quoted in the *Catechism of the Catholic Church* (2nd. ed., London: Geoffrey Chapman 1999), paragraph 2448. This was issued under the name of its prefect Cardinal Joseph Ratzinger, now Pope Benedict XVI.

[3] We can see the beginning of this shift in the pontificate of Pope Benedict XV during the First World War (see Ashley Beck, *Benedict XV* [CTS B694]) and the key turning point was John XXIII's 1963 encyclical *Pacem in Terris* (CTS S 264) which declared that war was irrational, *alienum a ratione*. This anti-war stance was further developed in the Second Vatican Council's Pastoral Constitution on the Church in the Modern World, *Gaudium et Spes* (CTS Do 724) and the teachings of Paul VI and John Paul II, together with their categorical opposition to the Vietnam War and both Gulf wars.

[4] New York: Harper and brothers, 1952, p. 15

[5] *Ibid.*, p. 21.

[6] *From Union Square to Rome*, in Day, *Selected Writings* (ed. R. Ellsberg, London: Darton, Longman and Todd 2005), p. 11.

[7] Quoted in William D. Miller, *Dorothy Day A Biography* (San Francisco: Harper and Row, 1982), p. 19.

[8] The novelist Sinclair Lewis (1885-1951) was the first American to win the Nobel prize for Literature. His best known novels are *Main Street*, *Babbitt* and *Arrowsmith* and he dealt with themes such as the place of women, race and the powerless in society. He has been called 'the conscience of his generation and he could well be the conscience of our own' (Sheldon Norman Grebstein)

[9] '....I walked the streets at sunset gazing at the clouds over Lincoln Park, recognizing the world as supremely beautiful, yet oppressed somehow with a heavy and abiding sense of loneliness and sadness...When what I read made me particularly class-conscious, I used to turn from the park with all its beauty and peacefulness and walk

down to North Avenue and over west through slum districts, and watch the slatterly women and the unkempt children and ponder over the poverty of the homes as contrasted with the wealth along the shore drive. I wanted even then to play my part. I wanted to write such books that thousands upon thousands of readers would be convinced of the injustice of things as they were.' (*From Union Square to Rome*, in *Selected Writings* p. 13)

[10] *Ibid.*, p. 15; also in *The Long Loneliness* (San Francisco: HarperCollins, 1997), p. 45. She was also influenced by the works of Jack London and Upton Sinclair.

[11] *The Long Loneliness* p. 63

[12] *Ibid.*, pp. 49-50.

[13] 'I felt the exultation, the joyous sense of the victory of the masses as they sang….the workers' hymn of Russia:

Arise, ye prisoners of starvation!
Arise, ye wretched of the earth!
For justice thunders condemnation
A better world's in birth.
No more tradition's chains shall bind us,
No more enslaved, no more enthralled,
The earth shall rise on new foundations.
We have been naught, we shall be all.
'Tis the final conflict,
Let each stand in his place….
The international working class
Shall be the human race.'

(Jim Forest, *Love is the Measure A Biography of Dorothy Day* (Basingstoke: Marhsall Pickering, 1987), p. 29

[14] *Ibid.*, pp.27-28 (with picture). See also Day's tribute to her when she died in *Selected Writings* pp.144ff.

[15] Pp. 54-56. See also the article 'Anarchism' written by Kropotkin for *The Encyclopaedia Britannica* 1910, available online from: *http://flag.blackened.net' daver/anarchism/kropotkin/defanarchy.html.*

[16] See Pontifical Council for Justice and Peace, *Compendium of the Social Doctrine of the Church* (London: Continuum, 2004), chapter 8.

[17] *Ibid.*, pp. 80-81.

[18] *Ibid.*, p. 85.

[19] The playwright Eugene O'Neill, (1888-1953), Pulitzer prize winner and one of the most important American dramatists of the 20th century, author of *Mourning Becomes Electra* and many other works. There is evidence that Day herself was strongly attracted to O'Neill at this time (See Miller, *op. cit.*, chapter 4). In *From Union Square to Rome* she quotes this extract from the poem:

'I fled him, down the nights and down the days,

I fled him, down in the arches of the years,

I fled him, down the labyrinthine ways

Of my own mind, and in the mist of ears

I hid from him.'

[20] *Ibid.*, p. 84. Day's friend Agnes Boulton, who later married O'Neill, 'quickly realised that Dorothy was subject to "sudden and unexplainable impulses" which drew her "into any nearby Catholic Church."' (Forest, *op. cit.*, p. 41) O'Neill shared and understood her religious longings.

[21] 'It was while staying in a room in Greenwich Village that she was dragged unconscious after another resident smelled gas coming from under her door. Whether it was by despair or accident is unclear, but the hose to a gas heater had been disconnected.' (*Ibid.*, p. 49) Miller is skeptical in his biography, but she refers to it in at least one letter.

[22] Miller says in the introduction to his biography that Day gave him, rather reluctantly, a rare copy. It is not in the British Library.

[23] Forest, *op. cit.*, p. 50.

[24] That might not have been the main reason for the break-up – by the time he died in 1964 Tobey had been married eight times.

[25] A. Mitchell Palmer was President Woodrow Wilson's Attorney General. In the years following the passing of the Deportation Act in 1918 between six and ten thousand people were arrested in raids which took place largely in eastern cities, designed to round up and deport 'aliens' who were involved in communist and anarchist activity, violating virtually every element of 'due process' supposedly protected in the US constitution. See *www.crf-usa.org/terror/PalmerRedRaids.htm.*

[26] Quoted in Miller, *op. cit.*, p. 163.

[27] No film was ever made. It looks as if the film makers really wanted the title, but they did not even make another film with that either.

[28] *Selected Writings*, introduction by R. Ellsberg, p. xxiii.

[29] *The Long Loneliness* p. 134.

[30] Tamar means 'little palm tree' in Hebrew, and Day says shat she was inspired in the choice by a friend, not knowing of the Tamars in the Old Testament; the second name reflects her reading about St Teresa of Avila (*Ibid.*, pp. 140-1).

[31] She was also reading *The Imitation of Christ* and William James' book *The Varieties of Religious Experience*.

[32] *Ibid.*, p. 137.

[33] *Ibid.*, p. 138.

[34] *Ibid.*, p. 142.

[35] *Ibid.*, pp. 143-4.

[36] 'Forster saw man in the light of reason and not in the light of faith. He had thought of the baptism only as a mumbo jumbo, the fuss and flurry peculiar to women. At first he had been indulgent and had brought in the lobsters for the feast. And then he had become angry with some sense of the end to which all this portended. Jealousy set in and he left me.' (*Ibid.*, p. 144)

[37] *Ibid.*, pp. 145-147. The trial and the execution was a notorious event in the history of America in the 1920s. It is generally thought that the evidence on which they were convicted of murder was very weak, and that the state's desire for an execution in the politically charge atmosphere of the time, was the driving force in the men's death. There were riots all over the world after the execution, and Vanzetti's prison writings became a classic. Principled opposition to the death penalty was a consistent mark of Day's life, now (but not in the 1920s) reflected in the clear teachings of the Catholic Church (see Pope John Paul II, *Evangelium Vitae* [1998, CTS Do 633] 56, and *Catechism of the Catholic Church* [revised edition, London: Chapman, 1999], 2266).

[38] Although she had been baptised in the Episcopal Church as a child it was the custom in this period for virtually all converts from other churches to be baptised conditionally, which is not the case today unless there is genuine cause for doubt as the validity of the baptism.

Confirmation was generally received by converts at a later stage, in Day's case at Pentecost the following year at the Convent of the Holy Souls on 85th Street.

[39] *Ibid.*, p. 148. There was more joy when she was confirmed.

[40] *Selected Writings*, introduction by Ellsberg, p. xxiv.

[41] *The Long Loneliness* p. 149.

[42] Day says that she wanted to put off returning to New York because she still hungered for Forster Batterham, and wanted to avoid the occasions of sin.

[43] *Ibid.*, p. 165.

[44] *Ibid.*, p. 166.

[45] Day's words quoted by Miller, *op. cit.*, p. 248 = *Peter Maurin* p. 91.

[46] Peter Maurin spoke little of his life before Day encountered him. *Peter Maurin Apostle to the World* (Maryknoll: Orbis, 2004) is a reworking of biographical material put together by her before his death, but never completed or published, by Professor Francis Sicius.

[47] *The Long Loneliness* p. 169.

[48] Also, 'a red-headed Irish Communist in Union Square told me to see you. He says we think alike.' (*Ibid.*)

[49] In addition to his work there is a brief biography of Maurin by Jim Forest on the Catholic Worker website, *www.catholicworker.org*. Marc Ellis, *Peter Maurin: Prophet in the Twentieth Century* (New York: Paulist Press, 1981) has been reprinted by the Catholic Worker Bookshop in Washington, DC, *http://www.catholicworker.com/bookstore/index.html*. There have been several dissertations and theses as well.

[50] At various stages in his life the spelling of some of his names varies, possibly to avoid conscription.

[51] *Peter Maurin* pp. 6ff., with photographs of the village today.

[52] CTS Do 680. See Rodger Charles SJ *Christian Social Witness and Teaching* volume 2 (Leominster: Gracewing 1998), pp. 15-30.

[53] See *Peter Maurin* pp. 10-12.

[54] Sangnier called for 'the reconciliation of Christ and the people, of Catholicism and the suffering of the revolutionary masses.' (quoted in Oscar Cole Arnal, article on Marc Sangnier and Sillon in Judith A.

Dwyer [ed.] *The New Dictionary of Catholic Social Thought* [Collegeville: The Liturgical Press, 1994], p. 860.) The movement was effectively suppressed by Pope St Pius X in 1910.

[55] He later said,' Sillon was full of enthusiasm and generosity, but lacked deep thought. It allowed itself to present democracy as the only political regime in conformity with Christianity. It was condemned for the preceding reason as well as imprudence in thought and action' quoted in Pete Maurin p. 18.

[56] *Ibid.*, pp. 19ff. on how and why this enterprise failed.

[57] *Ibid.*, p. 30.

[58] *Ibid.*, p. 37.

[59] 'Peter was vehemently opposed to the wage system, so he received in return for his labour, which he pointed out was voluntarily "given", the return "gift" of enough food and clothing… …he never had more than the clothes on his back, but he took the Gospel counsel literally – "If anyone asks for thy coat give him thy cloak too". That is, if he encountered anyone needing a oat, and he had already given his own away, he would take the person to some friend and ask for a coat for him. He went in all simplicity to men like Thomas Woodlock of the *Wall Street Journal* and not asked them for things, but also discussed finance capitalism, unemployment and usury with them.' (*The Long Loneliness* pp. 178-9).

[60] *Ibid.*, pp. 179-180. This was how he answered a question in a radio interview about the answer to unemployment: 'Feed the hungry for Christ's sake, clothe the naked for Christ's sake, as the first Christians used to do, which made the pagans say about the Christians, "See how they love one another."' (quoted in Miller, *op. cit.*, p. 281.

[61] Another favourite was his wish to 'make the encyclicals click'.

[62] For a discussion of the encyclical see Charles, *op. cit.*, pp. 63-71.

[63] *Ibid.*, p. 171.

[64] *Ibid.*, pp. 172-3.

[65] *Ibid.*, p. 187.

[66] See *Selected Writings* pp. 132ff., from *Loaves and Fishes*.

[67] See M. Piehl, *Breaking Bread The Catholic Worker movement and the origin of the Catholic Radical Movement in America* (Philadelphia:

Temple University Press, 1982). Illustrating Maurin's scorn for state welfare Piehl quotes him saying, 'Once the poor had been fed and clothed by the Christians as a personal sacrifice, and society had said of them, "See how they love each other." Now the poor were handed over to the state, and society said about Christians, "See how they pass the buck."' (p. 115) Most commentators think that the war inevitably relegated the Catholic Worker movement to the margins of Catholic intellectual life, away from the mainstream, because of its pacifism.

[68] Not for the last time, Day respectfully criticised the Archbishop of New York, Cardinal Francis Spellman, who had made a speech attacking the strikers. She wrote to him: 'This is so far your only statement, which has certainly not been a fair statement to the workers, and has been aimed at alienating any sympathy for them. I am sure you did not intend it in this way, and that you have been misinformed. I am writing to you because this strike, though small, is a terribly significant one in a way. It is not just the issue of wages and hours, as I can see from the conversations our Catholic Workers have with them. It is a question of their dignity as men. You are a prince of the Church, and a great man in the eyes of the world, and your opponents are all little men, hard working day labourers filled with grievances. They want to talk to you, and, oh, I do beg you so much with al my heart to go to them…It is easier for the great to give in than the poor…' (quoted in Piehl, *op. cit.*, p.93)

[69] *Catholic Worker* September 1960 in *Selected Writings* p. 194. The principle of love of brother, made real in voluntary poverty, meant that Day challenged people at all levels about the jobs they should do in life: 'If our jobs do not contribute to the common good, we pray God for the grace to give them up. Have they to do with shelter, food, clothing? Have they to do with the works of Mercy? Everyone should be able to place his job in the category of the Works of Mercy. This would exclude jobs in advertising, which only increases people's useless desires, and in insurance companies and banks, which are known to exploit the poor of this country and of others. Whatever has contributed to the misery and degradation of the poor may be considered a bad job, and not to be worked at. If we examined our consciences in this way we would soon

be driven into manual labour, into humble work, and so would become more like Our Lord and our Blessed Mother.' (from 'December' in *On Pilgrimage* [1949] in *Selected Writings* p. 229)

[70] 'Maurin believed, as do current ecologists, that in the modern era the quest for productivity and profit replaced healthy concern for the soil. To counteract this, he proposed an agricultural system that began with respect for creation, which in this case meant the soil. He believed that Catholicism, representing a philosophy rooted in the land, provided the best preparation for such a system.' (Peter Maurin p. 128)

[71] See 'Mr O'Connell', an obituary of Maurice O'Connell, who made the wooden furniture for the chapel at the farm at Easton, which also describes vividly how the place functioned as a retreat centre, *Catholic Worker* March 1952, in *Selected Writings* pp. 127-132.

[72] *The Long Loneliness* pp. 228-9.

[73] 'The Mystical Body of Christ' *Catholic Worker*, October 1939.

[74] William Cavanaugh, in *Torture and Eucharist* (Oxford: Blackwell 1999), p. 221, contrasts Day's theology of the Mystical Body with that of Pope Pius XII in his encyclical *Mystici Corporis Christi* (1943, CTS Do 266) – his understanding is that being part of the Body of Christ unites Christians even though they are engaged in conflict with each other: it does not prevent the conflict from happening. He writes: 'It is not difficult to sympathise with Pius's efforts to bring some hope of communion to a world riven with strife. Nevertheless, one can imagine that the Pope's words would be slight comfort to the Christian on the battlefield who finds that a fellow member of the mystical body of Christ is trying to blow his legs off.' (pp. 211-212).

[75] She wrote: 'Christians, when they are seeking to defend their faith by arms, by force and violence, are like those who said to Our Lord, "Come down from the Cross. If you are the Son of God, save Yourself." But Christ did not come down from the Cross. He drank to the last drop the agony of His suffering, and was not part of the agony the hopelessness, the unbelief, of His own disciples?....If 2,000 have suffered martyrdom in Spain, is that suffering atoned for by the death of the 90,000 in the Civil War? Would not these martyrs themselves have cried out against more shedding of blood? Prince of Peace, Christ our

King, Christ our Brother, Christ the Son of Man, have mercy on us and give us the courage to suffer…' (*Catholic Worker* November 1936, in *Selected Writings* p. 78)

[76] *The Long Loneliness* p. 206. Unfortunately when the High school students, after this massive demonstration of more than two thousand people, went on to get involved in the Catholic Worker's support for a strike by workers for the National Biscuit Company, and started boycotting its products, the school authorities withdrew their support for the movement and stopped the school's bulk order for copies of the paper.

[77] 'Christian Action in World Crisis' in Thomas Merton, *Passion for Peace* ed. William H. Shannon (New York: Crossroad 1996), p.91, originally in *Blackfriars*, June 1962.

[78] *Catholic Worker* January 1942, in *Selected Writings* pp. 261-2.

[79] The bombings were condemned by Pope Pius XII, who pointed out that 'every act of war directed at the indiscriminate destruction of whole cities or vast areas with their inhabitants is a crime against God and man.' *L'Osservatore Romano*, (7 August 1945): 'This war provides a catastrophic conclusion. Incredibly this destructive weapon remains as a temptation for posterity, which, we know by bitter experience, learns so little from history.' The magazine *Commonweal* (for which Day often wrote, like Merton) wrote that 'Hiroshima and Nagasaki are names for American guilt and shame.' In England, one of the few religious figures to speak out was Mgr Ronald Knox, in *God and the Atom* (London: Sheed and Ward, 1945). Note also the protest of the Catholic philosopher Elizabeth Anscombe against the award of an honorary degree by Oxford University to President Truman and her contribution and that of her husband Peter Geach in William Stein (ed.), *Nuclear Weapons and Christian Conscience* (London: Methuen 1961). Other European and American intellectuals in the Catholic Church in the 50s and 60s opposed to nuclear weapons were Pierre Regamey, James Douglass, Bede Griffiths OP, the psychologist Karl Stern, and E. I. Watkin (the pioneer of the 'Guild of the Pope's Peace in the First World War). See also J. Siemes SJ *The Day the Bomb Fell* (1984, CTS S373)

[80] *Catholic Worker* September 1945, in *Selected Writings* pp. 266 – 268. Truman was a Freemason.

[81] 'Peter's Death', *The Long Loneliness* pp. 273-281.

[82] For example, the collection edited by Walter Stein cited in note 79 above was entirely made up of contributions by lay Catholic academics (although the preface was written by a retired Jesuit archbishop, Thomas Roberts). Even as late as the 1980s much of the academic critique of deterrence was still led by lay Catholics, as in J. Finnis, J. Boyle and G. Grisez, *Nuclear Deterrence, Morality and Realism* (Oxford 1987). The present Holy Father's World Peace Day message for 2006 has greatly strengthened Catholic opposition to nuclear weapons and policies of nuclear deterrence,

http://www.vatican.va/holy_father/benedict_xvi/mesages/peace/docume nts?hf_be-xvi_mes_20051213_xxxix-world-day-peace_en.html. See also *Compendium of the Social Doctrine of the Church* (London: Continuum 2005), paragraph 508.

[83] CTS S 264. War is condemned as irrational, *alienum a ratione* (126-127)

[84] See 'We go on record', extracts from *Catholic Worker* articles in 1972 in Selected Writings pp. 311-317.

[85] CTS Do 724.

[86] See Peter Hebblethwaite *Paul VI The First Modern Pope* (London: HarperCollins 1993), chapter 29. The pope was not backed by Cardinal Spellman or many of the American bishops.

[87] CTS Do 273.

[88] *Catholic Worker* January 1967, in Selected Writings p. 338.

[89] *Catholic Worker* July – August 1961, December 1961, July - August 1962, September 1962, November 1962, December 1962 in *Selected Writings* pp.298ff.

[90] The farm, founded by the Baptist minister Clarence Jordan, is still there; see *http://www.koinoniapartners.org*.

[91] *Catholic Worker* September 1973, in *Selected Writings* p. 257.

[92] In her open letter to Fr Dan Berrigan SJ (*Catholic Worker* December 1972, in *Selected Writings* pp. 346-8), at the time of his brother Philip's imprisonment and decision to leave the priesthood, she laments the

decline in confession and reiterates traditional teaching about birth control, abortion and divorce.

[93] Miller, *op. cit.*, p. 513.

[94] *Selected Writings* pp. 354ff. contains reflections in the *Catholic Worker* about the psalms, the paper and movement's constant need for financial support and the election of Pope John Paul II.

[95] *Selected Writings*, p. xi.

[96] From *The Third Hour* (1949) in *Selected Writings* p. 102.

[97] 'By pretending to test who will receive the benefit and who will not you may possibly neglect some who are beloved of God' quoted in Piehl, *op. cit.*, p. 105.

[98] She reflected that the farm on Staten Island would have been self-supporting in terms of the bread produced there if it was not all given away.

[99] As set out in Anders Nygren, *Agape and Eros* (New York: Harper and Row, 1969). Day's approach is analysed in depth in Mary Louise Bozza, *Dorothy Day: On Love of God, Neighbour and Self* (Dissertation for BA Honors programme, Boston College, 2003 – see reading list for how to access the dissertation online)

[100] 'December', from *On Pilgrimage* (1949) in *Selected Writings* p. 231.

[101] *Catholic Worker* June 1935 in Scott, *op.cit.*, p. 34.;

[102] *Catholic Worker* April 1935, *ibid.*, pp. 31-32.

[103] She was positive about some things, such as the occasional use of guitars or trumpets, but disliked constant innovation for its own sake and Masses geared to particular groups (*Catholic Worker* May 1967 in Scott, *op.cit.*, pp. 96-98). She did not approve of Mass said with a chalice that looked like a coffee cup.

[104] *The Long Loneliness* p. 133. The statue was presumably the one from Czechoslovakia given to her by her friend and former fellow-prisoner Peggy Baird (*The Commonweal* 5 November 1943 = *Selected Writings* p. 160).

[105] *Ibid.*, pp. 161-2.

[106] *Thérèse* Springfield: Templegate 1979, but published originally by Fides Publishers in 1960; extracts are in *Selected Writings* pp. 187-203. See also *Thérèse of Lisieux*, CTS B 204.

[107] 'I'm not trying to say that the Little Flower would have out on picket lines and spoken on communist platforms…she was a product of her environment, bourgeois, middle class, the daughter of skilled workers, frugal people who lived part from the world with their eyes on God….' *Catholic Worker* April 1952, in Scott, op.cit., pp. 119-120.

[108] *Selected Writings* p. 201. This description contrasts with the misleading sentimentality which sometimes surrounds devotion to St Thérèse.

[109] The groups such as the 'Wobblies' to which she belonged were basically communist in outlook, she was never actually a member of the Communist Party of America.

[110] I am grateful to the Anglican theologian Fr Ken Leech for this information.

[111] Quoted in Scott, *op.cit.*, p. 23.

[112] *Acts* 5:38.

[113] *Catholic Worker* May 2000, in the 'Catholic Worker Home Page', *http://www.catholicworker.com* which enlarges on this basic statement, detailing the movement's teachings.

[114] St Francis House, Oxford Catholic Worker, 227 Cowley Road, Oxford OX4 1XG, telephone 01685 248288. Their publication is called *Strangers and Pilgrims*.

[115] *http://www.londoncatholicworker.org/DDhouse.htm*, which gives a fuller description of the house and those who are based there.

[116] *http://www.londoncatholicworker.org/CWfarm.htm*, which also gives more details about the farm and opportunities for volunteers and interns.

[117] Available online from *www.londoncatholicworker.org* or from 14 Deal Street, London E1 5AH, email *londoncatholicworker@yahoo.co.uk* where other material is to be found.

[118] See *http://www.simoncommunity.org.uk*.

Europe's Soul and her Patron Saints

To build Europe on solid foundations, economic interests may not be enough. This booklet makes a measured assessment of the immensely rich Christian heritage of modern Europe, through the prism of Europe's six patron saints, and draws timeless lessons and values that can guide Catholics and others in their thinking about Europe today. The current battle for Europe's soul, anticipated by its founding fathers themselves, is one on which all Christians should be well informed.

Fr Beck is Assistant Priest of Beckenham, in the diocese of Southwark, and Dean of Studies of the Permanent Diaconate Formation Programme for ten dioceses in southern England and Wales.

ISBN: 978 1 86082 442 5

CTS Code: Do758

Oscar Romero

Gunned down while saying Mass at the height of political and social unrest in El Salvador, Oscar Romero has remained a controversial and often misunderstood figure. Fr Beck shows how he was not martyred for political activism, or simply for being 'on the side of the poor', but for his faithfulness to Christ and his Church. Romero's impressive body of teaching, his own personal holiness, and sufferings, are thoroughly explored here, and clearly illustrate what - as Pope Benedict has said - 'an important witness to the faith' he truly was.

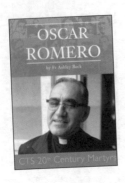

Fr Beck is Assistant Priest of Beckenham, in the diocese of Southwark, and Dean of Studies of the Permanent Diaconate Formation Programme for ten dioceses in southern England and Wales.

ISBN: 978 1 86082 485 2

CTS Code: B700